GOOD OL' SONGS

MELODY LINE, CHORDS AND LYRICS
FOR KEYBOARD • GUITAR • VOCAL

HAL•LEONARD®

ISBN 0-634-01831-0

HAL•LEONARD®
CORPORATION
7777 W. BLUEMOUND RD. P.O. BOX 13819 MILWAUKEE, WI 53213

Visit Hal Leonard Online at
www.halleonard.com

Welcome to the PAPERBACK SONGS SERIES.

Do you play piano, guitar, electronic keyboard, sing or play any instrument for that matter? If so, this handy "pocket tune" book is for you.

The concise, one-line music notation consists of:

MELODY, LYRICS & CHORD SYMBOLS

Whether strumming the chords on guitar, "faking" an arrangement on piano/keyboard or singing the lyrics, these fake book style arrangements can be enjoyed at any experience level – hobbyist to professional.

The musical skills necessary to successfully use this book are minimal. If you play guitar and need some help with chords, a basic chord chart is included at the back of the book.

While playing and singing is the first thing that comes to mind when using this book, it can also serve as a compact, comprehensive reference guide.

However you choose to use this PAPERBACK SONGS SERIES book, by all means have fun!

CONTENTS

(contents continued)

ABA DABA HONEYMOON

Words and Music by
ARTHUR FIELDS and WALTER DONOVAN

Moderately

"Ab-a, dab-a, dab-a, dab-a dab-a, dab-a, dab," said the

Chim-pie to the Monk. "Bab-a, dab-a, dab-a, dab-a,

dab-a, dab-a, dab," said the Mon-key to the

Chimp. All night long they'd chat-ter a-way,

all day long they're hap-py and gay, —

swing — ing and sing — ing in their

hon-key, ton-key way.

9

AFTER THE BALL
from A TRIP TO CHINATOWN

Words and Music by
CHARLES K. HARRIS

Fast Waltz

A   lit - tle   maid - en
"Bright   lights   were   flash - ing
"Long   years   have   passed,   child;

climbed   an   old   man's   knee, _____
in   the   grand   ball - room, _____
I've   nev - er   wed, _____

Begged   for   a   sto - ry,
Soft - ly   the   mu - sic,
True   to   my   lost   love,

"Do,   un - cle, please! _____
play - ing   sweet   tunes, _____
through   she   is   dead. _____

Why   are   you   sin - gle;
There   came   my   sweet - heart,
She   tried   to   tell   me,

E7   Am

why	live	a -	lone? _____
my	love,	my	own, _____
tried	to	ex -	plain; _____

C   G

Have	you	no	ba -	bies,
'I	wish	some	wa -	ter;
I	would	not	lis -	ten,

A7   D7   G

have	you	no	home?" _____
leave	me	a -	lone.' _____
plead -	ings	were	vain. _____

Em   Am   B7

"I	had	a	sweet -	heart,
When	I	re -	turned,	dear,
One	day	a	let -	ter

C   G

years,	years	a -	go;
there	stood	a	man, _____
came	from	that	man; _____

C   G

Where	she	is	now,	pet,
Kiss -	ing	my	sweet -	heart,
He	was	her	broth -	er,

12

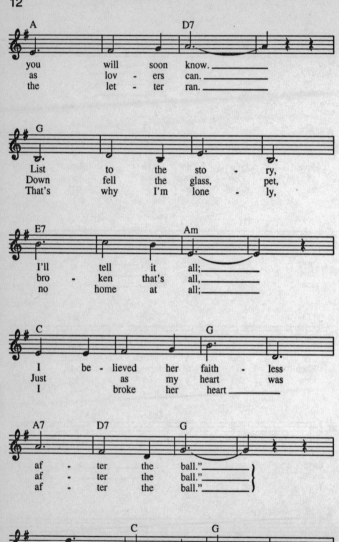

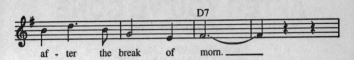

af - ter the break of morn._____

Af - ter the danc - ers' leav - ing;

Af - ter the stars are gone;_____

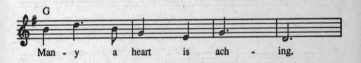

Man - y a heart is ach - ing,

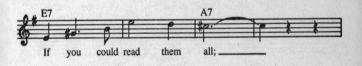

If you could read them all;_____

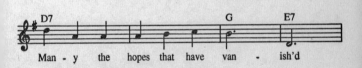

Man - y the hopes that have van - ish'd

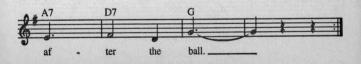

af - ter the ball._____

AFTER YOU'VE GONE
from ONE MO' TIME

Words by HENRY CREAMER
Music by TURNER LAYTON

A7   Dm   A7

when you'll re - gret it;   Some   day,
all kinds of weath - er;   Some   day,

Dm   Fm

when you grow lone -   ly,
blue and down - heart -   ed,

C   E7

your heart will break like mine and
you'll long to be with me right

Am   D7

you'll want me on -   ly,
back where you start -   ed;

C

Af - ter you've gone, ____
Af - ter I'm gone, ____

G7   C

Af - ter you've gone a - way. ____
Af - ter I'm gone a - way. ____

1
2

AIN'T WE GOT FUN?
from BY THE LIGHT OF THE SILVERY MOON

Words by GUS KAHN and RAYMOND B. EGAN
Music by RICHARD A. WHITING

ALABAMA JUBILEE

Words by JACK YELLEN
Music by GEORGE COBB

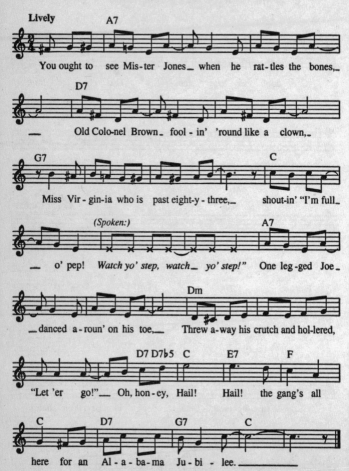

You ought to see Mis-ter Jones when he rat-tles the bones, Old Colo-nel Brown fool-in' 'round like a clown, Miss Vir-gin-ia who is past eight-y-three, shout-in' "I'm full o' pep! *Watch yo' step, watch yo' step!*" One leg-ged Joe danced a-roun' on his toe, Threw a-way his crutch and hol-lered, "Let 'er go!" Oh, hon-ey, Hail! Hail! the gang's all here for an Al-a-ba-ma Ju-bi-lee.

ALEXANDER'S RAGTIME BAND
from ALEXANDER'S RAGTIME BAND

Words and Music by
IRVING BERLIN

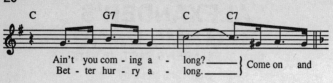

Ain't you com - ing a - long?
Bet - ter hur - ry a - long.
} Come on and

hear, Come on and hear Al - ex - an - der's Rag - time

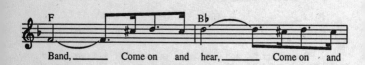

Band, Come on and hear, Come on and

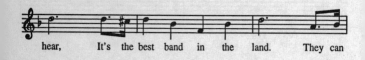

hear, It's the best band in the land. They can

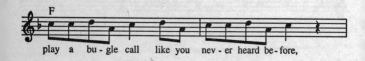

play a bu - gle call like you nev - er heard be - fore,

So nat - ur - al that you want to go to war;

That's just the best - est band what am,

ALICE BLUE GOWN
from IRENE

Lyric by JOSEPH McCARTHY
Music by HARRY TIERNEY

In my sweet lit - tle A - lice Blue Gown, _____ when I first wan - dered down in to town, _____ I was both proud and shy, as I felt ev - 'ry eye, but in ev - 'ry shop win - dow I'd primp, pass - ing

APRIL SHOWERS

from BOMBO

Words by B.G. DeSYLVA
Music by LOUIS SILVERS

With an easy flow

Though A - pril show - ers may come your way, they bring the flow - ers that bloom in May; so if it's rain - ing, have no re - grets be - cause it is - n't rain - ing rain you know, it's rain - ing vi - o -

AVALON

Words by AL JOLSON and B.G. DeSYLVA
Music by VINCENT ROSE

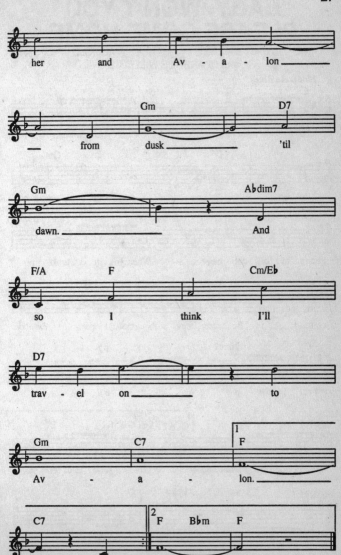

BABY, WON'T YOU PLEASE COME HOME

Words and Music by CHARLES WARFIELD
and CLARENCE WILLIAMS

BEALE STREET BLUES

Words and Music by
W.C. HANDY

Slowly

I've seen the lights of gay Broad-
The sev - en won - ders of the world I've

way, old Mar - ket
seen, and man - y

Street down by the Fris - co Bay.
are the pla - ces I have been.

I've strolled the Pra - do,
Take my ad - vice folks

I've gam - bled on the Bourse.
and see Beale Street first.

1.
2.
You'll

see pret - ty Browns in beau - ti - ful gowns. You'll see
see Hog - Nose res - t'rants and Chit - lin' Ca - fes. You'll see
see men who rank with the first in the na - tion, who
Beale Street could talk if Beale Street could talk mar - ried

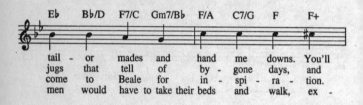

Eb   Bb/D   F7/C   Gm7/Bb   F/A   C7/G   F   F+

tail - or   mades and   hand   me   downs. You'll
jugs   that   tell   of   by - gone   days, and
come   to   Beale for   in - spi - ra - tion.
men   would   have to take their beds   and   walk,   ex -

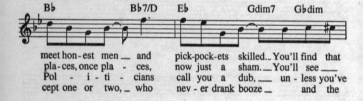

Bb   Bb7/D   Eb   Gdim7   Gbdim

meet hon - est men   and   pick-pock-ets skilled. You'll find that
pla - ces, once pla - ces,   now just a   sham. You'll see
Pol - i - ti - cians   call you a   dub,   un - less you've
cept one or two,   who   nev - er drank booze   and the

Bb/F   [1 - 3]   F7   Bb

bus'-ness nev - er clos - es till some - bod - y gets killed. You'll
Gold - en Balls e - nough to pave the New Je - ru - sa - lem. You'll
been in - i - ti - a - ted in the Rick - ri - ters Club. If
blind man on the cor - ner who

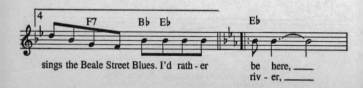

[4]   F7   Bb Eb   Eb

sings the Beale Street Blues. I'd rath - er   be   here,
river,

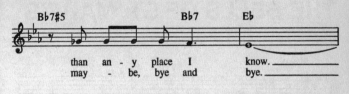

Bb7#5   Bb7   Eb

than an - y place I   know. ____
may - be, bye and   bye. ____

Eb7   Ab

____ I'd rath - er be here ____
____ Goin' to the riv - er, ____

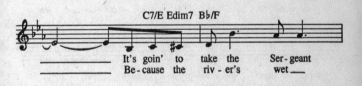

Ab7   Eb

than an - y place I   know. ____
and there's a rea - son why. ____

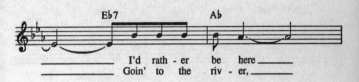

C7/E Edim7 Bb/F

____ It's goin' to take the Ser - geant
____ Be - cause the riv - er's wet ____

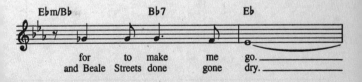

Ebm/Bb   Bb7   Eb

for to make me go. ____
and Beale Streets done gone dry. ____

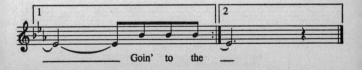

1   2

____ Goin' to the ____

THE BELLS OF ST. MARY'S

Words by DOUGLAS FURBER
Music by A. EMMETT ADAMS

BY THE LIGHT OF THE SILVERY MOON

Lyrics by ED MADDEN
Music by GUS EDWARDS

BILL BAILEY, WON'T YOU PLEASE COME HOME

Words and Music by
HUGHIE CANNON

BY THE BEAUTIFUL SEA

Words by HAROLD R. ATTERIDGE
Music by HARRY CARROLL

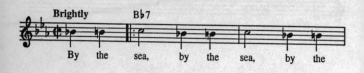

By the sea, by the sea, by the

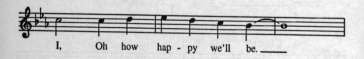

beau - ti - ful sea ___ you and I, you and

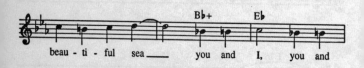

I, Oh how hap - py we'll be. ___

When each wave comes a - roll - ing

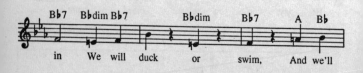

in We will duck or swim, And we'll

37

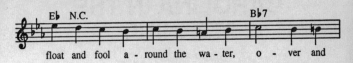

float and fool a - round the wa - ter, o - ver and

un - der and then up for air. ___ Pa is

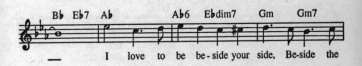

rich, Ma is rich, so now what do we care? ___

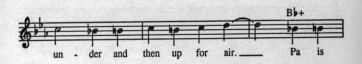

___ I love to be be - side your side, Be - side the

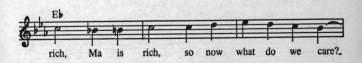

sea, be - side the sea - side, ___ by the beau - ti - ful

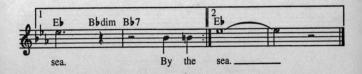

sea.   By the sea. ___

CAROLINA IN THE MORNING

Lyrics by GUS KAHN
Music by WALTER DONALDSON

(1.,D.C.) Noth - ing could be fin - er than to
(2.) Stroll - ing with my girl - ie where the

be in Car - o - li - na in the morn -
dew is pearl - y ear - ly in the morn -

ing, No one could be sweet - er than my
ing, But - ter - flies all flut - ter up and

sweet - heart when I meet her in the
kiss each lit - tle but - ter - cup at

morn - ing.
dawn -

Where the morn - ing glo - ries

twine a - round the door,

D7 G E7
Whis - per - ing pret - ty sto - ries
Am D7 G7 D.C. al Coda
I long to hear once more.
CODA
G7 C
ing. If I had A - lad - din's lamp for
C7
on - ly a day,
F D7 G7
I'd make a wish and here's what I'd say:
C
Noth - ing could be fin - er than to
be in Car - o - li - na in the
D7 G7 C
morn - ing.

CHICAGO
(That Toddlin' Town)

Words and Music by
FRED FISHER

41

CHINATOWN,
MY CHINATOWN

Words by WILLIAM JEROME
Music by JEAN SCHWARTZ

CIRIBIRIBIN

**Words and Music by
ANTONIO PESTALOZZA**

Su fi - ni - sci - la coi ba - ci____ Bel Mo-
I am wait-ing here for you____ love____ as the

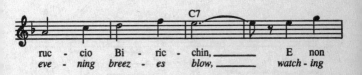

ruc - cio Bi - ric - chin,_____ E non
eve - ning breez - es blow,_____ watch-ing

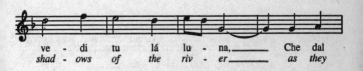

ve - di tu lá lu - na,_____ Che dal
shad - ows of the riv - er_____ as they

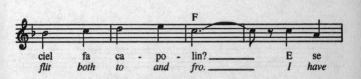

ciel fa ca - po - lin?_____ E se
flit both to and fro._____ I have

pur la lu - na spi - a____ Noi la-
come to see the love - light____ danc-ing

44

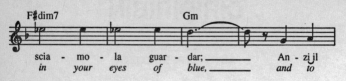

scia - mo - la guar - dar; _____ An - zi jl
in your eyes of blue, _____ and to

pal - li - do suo rag - gio _____ Ci con -
hear you soft - ly whis - per _____ that to

si - glia - a se - gui - tar! _____ Ci - ri - bi - ri -
me _____ you'll e'er be true. _____ Ci - ri - bi - ri -

bin, Ci - ri - bi - ri - bin, Ci - ri - bi - ri - bin. _____ Ci - ri - bi - ri -
bin, Ci - ri - bi - ri - bin, Ci - ri - bi - ri - bin. _____ Ci - ri - bi - ri -

bin, che bel fac - cin, Che squar - do
bin, the moon looks down up - on our

dol - ce ed as - sas - sin! _____ Ci - ri - bi - ri -
hap - pi - ness se - rene. _____ Ci - ri - bi - ri -

45

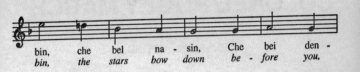

bin, che bel na - sin, Che bei den -
bin, *the* *stars* *bow* *down* *be - fore* *you,*

tin, che bel boc - chin! _____ Ci - ri - bi - ri -
tin, *O* *my* *ra - diant* *queen.* _____ *Ci - ri - bi - ri*

bin, che bel na - sin, Che bei den -
bin, *more* *love* *than* *mine* *for* *you* *the*

tin, che bel boc - chin! _____ Ci - ri - bi - ri -
world *has* *nev - er* *seen.* _____ *Ci - ri - bi - ri -*

bin, _____ Ci - ri - bi - ri - bin, _____ Ci - ri - bi - ri -
bin, _____ *Ci - ri - bi - ri - bin,* _____ *Ci - ri - bi - ri -*

bin, che bel boc - chin! _____
bin, *my* *ra - diant* *queen.* _____

COLONEL BOGEY MARCH

Music by
KENNETH J. ALFORD

CUDDLE UP A LITTLE CLOSER, LOVEY MINE

from THE THREE TWINS

Words by OTTO HARBACH
Music by KARL HOSCHNA

DANNY BOY
(Londonderry Air)

Words by FREDERICK EDWARD WEATHERLY
Traditional Irish Folk Melody

1. Oh, Dan-ny Boy, the pipes, the pipes are call - ing, _ from glen to
2. But if he come, when all the flow'rs are dy - ing, _ and I am

glen, and down the moun-tain side. _____ The sum-mer's
dead, as dead I well may be, _____ ye'll come and

gone, and all the ro - ses fall - ing, _____ It's you, it's
find the place where I am ly - ing, _____ and kneel and

you must go and I must bide.. But come ye back when sum-mer's in the
say an *A - ve* there for me; _ And I shall hear, tho' soft your tread a-

mead - ow, _____ or when the val - ley's hush'd and white with
bove_ me, _____ and all my dreams will warm and sweet - er

snow. _____ 'Tis I'll be there in sun-shine or in
be. _____ If you will not fail to tell me that you

shad - ow, _ oh, Dan-ny Boy, oh Dan-ny Boy, I love you so!
love_ me, _ then I shall sleep in peace un - til you come to me!

DARDANELLA

Words by FRED FISHER
Music by FELIX BERNARD and JOHNNY S. BLACK

Slowly

Down _____ be - side the Dar - da - nel - la
When _____ the Turk - ish sul - tan saw her

Bay, where Or - i - ent - al breez - es play,
eyes, oh, he was ta - ken by sur - prise,

there lives a lone-some maid, Ar - me - nian.
he said, "I'll buy her for my ha - rem."

By _____ the Dar - da - nelles with glow-ing
I _____ just told the sul - tan to be

eyes, she looks a - cross the seas and sighs,
nice, she can't be bought for an - y price.

and weaves her love spell so Si - re - nian.
She said to me she could-n't bear him.

Soon I shall re - turn to Turk - e - stan.
So be - neath the Or - i - en - tal moon,

52

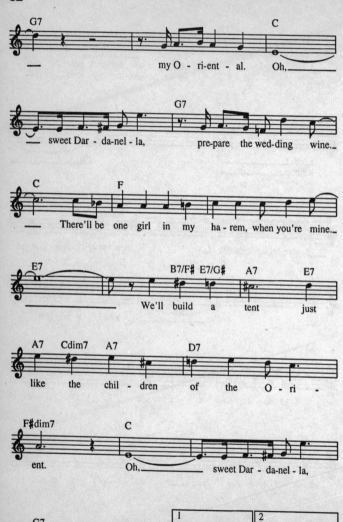

DARK EYES

Russian Cabaret Song

DOWN AMONG THE
SHELTERING PALMS

Words by JAMES BROCKMAN
Music by ABE OLMAN

Down ____ a-mong the shel-ter-ing palms _ oh hon-ey, wait for me ____ oh hon-ey wait for me. ____ Don't be ____ for-get-tin' we've got a date. ____ out where ____ the sun goes down a-bout eight. _ How my love ____ is burn-ing, burn-ing, burn-ing, how my heart ____ is yearn-ing, yearn-ing yearn-ing to be down ____ a-mong the shel-ter-ing palms, _ oh hon-ey, wait for me.

DOWN BY THE
OLD MILL STREAM

Words and Music by
TELL TAYLOR

Down by the old mill stream, _____ where I first met you, _____ with your eyes of blue, _____ dressed in ging - ham too. _____ It was there I knew, _____ that you loved me true, _____ you were six - teen, _____ my vil-lage queen, _____ by the old mill stream. Down by the stream. _____

DOWN YONDER

Words and Music by
L. WOLFE GILBERT

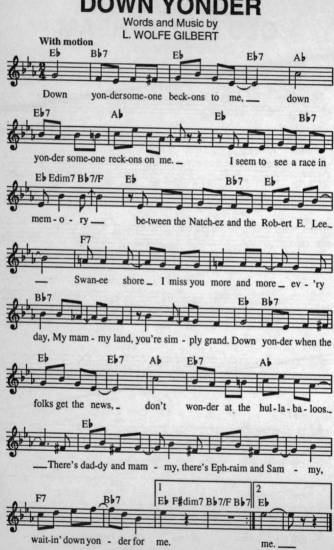

FASCINATION
(Valse Tzigane)
By F.D. MARCHETTI

THE ENTERTAINER

By SCOTT JOPLIN

Moderate Ragtime

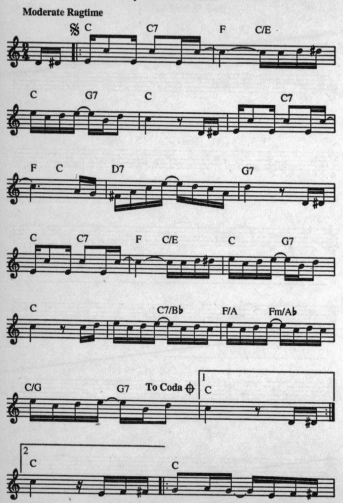

59

FOR HE'S A
JOLLY GOOD FELLOW

Traditional British Song

For he's a jol - ly good fel - low, for

he's a jol - ly good fel - low, for __

he's a jol - ly good fel - low, which

no - bod - y can de - ny. __

Which no - bod - y can de - ny, __ Which

no - bod - y can de - ny. __ For

FRANKIE AND JOHNNY

Anonymous Blues Ballad
possibly from St. Louis or Kansas City

1. Frank-ie and John-ny were lov-ers, said they were real-ly in
2. Frank-ie and John-ny went walk-ing, John-ny had on a new
3. John-ny said, "I've got to leave now, but I won't be ver-y
4. Frank-ie went down to the ho-tel, looked in the win-dow so
5. John-ny saw Frank-ie a-com-in'; down the back stairs he did
6. Frank-ie, she went to the big chair, calm as a la-dy could

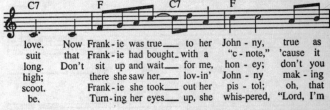

love. Now Frank-ie was true to her John-ny, true as
suit that Frank-ie had bought with a "c-note," 'cause it
long. Don't sit up and wait for me, hon-ey; don't you
high; there she saw her lov-in' John-ny mak-ing
scoot. Frank-ie she took out her pis-tol; oh, that
be. Turn-ing her eyes up, she whis-pered, "Lord, I'm

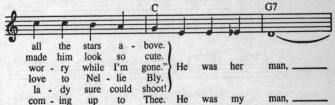

all the stars a-bove.
made him look so cute.
wor-ry while I'm gone." He was her man, _____
love to Nel-lie Bly.
la-dy sure could shoot!
com-ing up to Thee. He was my man, _____

1-5
_____ but he done her wrong. _____
6
_____ but he done me wrong." _____

FOR ME AND MY GAL
from FOR ME AND MY GAL

Words by EDGAR LESLIE and E. RAY GOETZ
Music by GEORGE W. MEYER

Moderately, with movement

THE GIRL I LEFT BEHIND ME

19th Century Irish

1. The ____ hour was sad I
2. Then ____ to the East we
3. Full ____ man - y a name our
4. The ____ hope of fi - nal
5. The ____ dames of France are

left the maid, A
bore a - way To
ban - ners bore Of
vic - to - ry With
fond and free, And

lin - g'ring fare - well ____ tak - ing, Her
win a name ____ in ____ sto - ry, And ____
for - mer deeds ____ of ____ dar - ing, But ____
in my bos - om ____ burn - ing Is ____
Flem - ish lips ____ are will - ing, And ____

sighs and tears my steps de - layed; I
there, where dawns of the sun of day, There
they where were of the days of yore, In
min - gled with sweet thoughts of thee, And
soft the maids of It - a - ly, While

65

GIVE MY REGARDS
TO BROADWAY

from LITTLE JOHNNY JONES
from YANKEE DOODLE DANDY

Words and Music by
GEORGE M. COHAN

Give my re-gards to Broad -

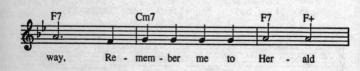

way, Re-mem-ber me to Her-ald

Square. _____ Tell all the

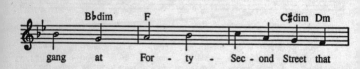

gang at For-ty - Sec-ond Street that

I will soon be there. _____

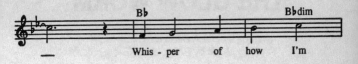

— Whis - per of how I'm

yearn - ing to min - gle with the

old time throng; _____

Give my re - gards to old Broad -

way and say that I'll be there ere

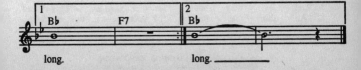

long.   long. _____

THE GLOW WORM

Words by LILLA CAYLEY ROBINSON
Music by PAUL LINCKE

Moderately

When the night falls si-lent-ly, __ the night falls
"Lit - tle glow - worm, tell me pray, __ oh glow-worm,

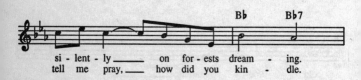

si - lent - ly _____ on for - ests dream - ing.
tell me pray, __ how did you kin - dle.

Lov - ers wan - der forth to see, __ they wan-der
Lamps that by the break of day, __ that by the

forth to see _____ the bright stars gleam - ing.
break of day, __ must fade and dwin - dle?"

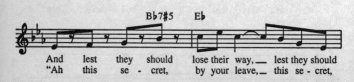

And lest they should lose their way, __ lest they should
"Ah this se - cret, by your leave, __ this se - cret,

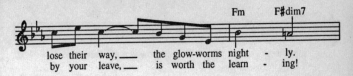

Fm   F#dim7

lose their way, ____ the glow-worms night - ly.
by your leave, ____ is worth the learn - ing!

Gm   D   Gm   C7   Bb

Light their ti - ny lan-terns gay, ____ their ti - ny
When true lov - ers come at eve, ____ true lov - ers

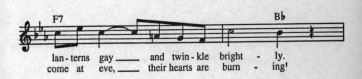

F7   Bb

lan - terns gay ____ and twin - kle bright - ly.
come at eve, ____ their hearts are burn - ing!

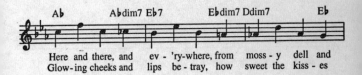

Ab   Abdim7 Eb7   Ebdim7 Ddim7   Eb

Here and there, and ev - 'ry-where, from moss - y dell and
Glow-ing cheeks and lips be - tray, how sweet the kiss - es

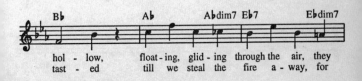

Bb   Ab   Abdim7 Eb7   Ebdim7

hol - low, float - ing, glid - ing through the air, they
tast - ed till we steal the fire a - way, for

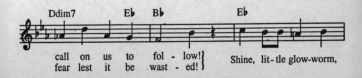

Ddim7   Eb Bb   Eb

call on us to fol - low!
fear lest it be wast - ed!   Shine, lit - tle glow-worm,

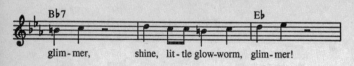

glim-mer, shine, lit-tle glow-worm, glim-mer!

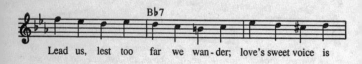

Lead us, lest too far we wan-der; love's sweet voice is

call-ing yon-der! Shine, lit-tle glow-worm, glim-mer,

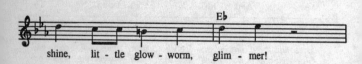

shine, lit-tle glow-worm, glim-mer!

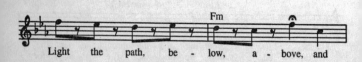

Light the path, be-low, a-bove, and

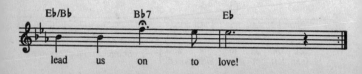

lead us on to love!

A GOOD MAN IS
HARD TO FIND

Words and Music by
EDDIE GREEN

GOOD NIGHT LADIES

Words by E.P. CHRISTY
Traditional Music

Moderately fast

Good night, la - dies, ___

Good night, la - dies! _ Good night,

la - dies, _ We're going to leave you now.

Mer - ri - ly we roll a - long, roll a - long, roll a - long.

Mer - ri - ly we roll a - long, O'er the deep blue sea.

GOODBYE, MY LADY LOVE

Words and Music by
JOSEPH E. HOWARD

Moderately fast

Good - bye, my la - dy love, Fare - well, my

tur - tle dove, You are the i - dol and

dar - ling of my heart, But some day you will come

back to me, and love me ten - der - ly, so

good-bye, my la - dy love, good - bye.

HAIL, HAIL, THE GANG'S ALL HERE

Words by D.A. ESROM
Music by THEODORE F. MORSE and ARTHUR SULLIVAN

Moderately

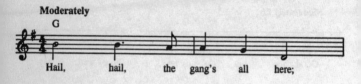

Hail, hail, the gang's all here;

what the heck do we care, what the heck do we care.

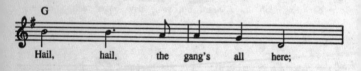

Hail, hail, the gang's all here;

what the heck do we care now!

HARRIGAN

from GEORGE M!

Words and Music by
GEORGE M. COHAN

HEARTS AND FLOWERS

Music by
THEODORE MOSES TOBANI

HELLO! MA BABY

Words by IDA EMERSON
Music by JOSEPH E. HOWARD

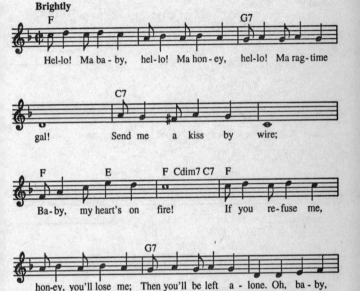

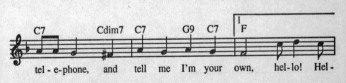

HINDUSTAN

Words and Music by OLIVER WALLACE and HAROLD WEEKS

(There'll Be)
A HOT TIME IN THE OLD TOWN TONIGHT

Words by JOE HAYDEN
Music by THEODORE M. METZ

I LOVE A PIANO
from the Stage Production STOP! LOOK! LISTEN!

Words and Music by
IRVING BERLIN

Eb   Bb7   Eb   Bb7   Eb   Bb7/F Eb/G

ped-al____ I love to med-dle.___ Not on-ly mu-sic from Broad-
(Orig: When Pa-de-rew-ski comes this

Eb   Eb7/G Eb7   Ab   Eb7

way.____   I'm so de-light-ed____   if I'm in-
way.)

Ab   Eb7   Ab Eb7/Bb Ab/C Ebdim Adim Gbdim7

vit-ed____ to hear a long haired gen - ius play.___ So you can

Bb7/F Bb7/Ab Gm D/F# Bb7/F   Bb7

keep   your   fid - dle   and your bow.__ Give me a

Cdim Bdim7 Bbdim7 Adim7 Abdim7 Eb/G   F7   Bb7

p - i - a - n - o.   Oh, oh, I love to

Eb   C7/E Bb7/F   Bb7   Eb   Bb7/F Eb/G F#dim

stop   right ____ be-side an up-right,   or a

F7   Bb7 |1 |2
                   | Eb Adim/Bb Bb7 | Eb

high toned ba-by   grand.   I love a   grand.

HOW 'YA GONNA KEEP 'EM DOWN ON THE FARM?
(After They've Seen Paree)

Words by SAM M. LEWIS and JOE YOUNG
Music by WALTER DONALDSON

harm? That's a mys - ter - y; _____

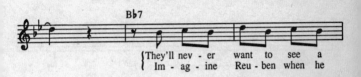

{ They'll nev - er want to see a
Im - ag - ine Reu - ben when he

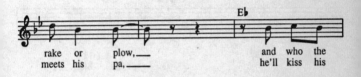

rake or plow, _____ and who the
meets his pa, _____ he'll kiss his

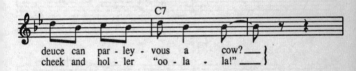

deuce can par - ley - vous a cow? _____ }
cheek and hol - ler "oo - la - la!" _____ }

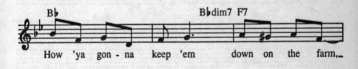

How 'ya gon - na keep 'em down on the farm, _____

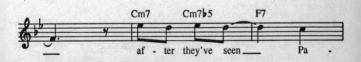

_____ af - ter they've seen _____ Pa -

ree?" _____ ree?" _____

I AIN'T GOT NOBODY
(And Nobody Cares for Me)

Words by ROGER GRAHAM
Music by SPENCER WILLIAMS and DAVE PEYTON

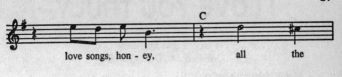

love songs, hon - ey, all the

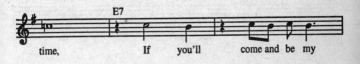

time, If you'll come and be my

sweet ba - by mine; 'Cause

I _____ ain't got no -

- bod - y, And __ no - bod - y

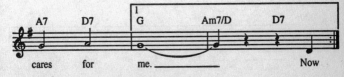

cares for me. _____ Now

me. _____

I LOVE YOU TRULY

Words and Music by
CARRIE JACOBS-BOND

I WANT A GIRL
(Just Like the Girl That Married Dear Old Dad)

Words by WILLIAM DILLON
Music by HARRY VON TILZER

When I was a boy__ my moth - er

oft - en said to me, __ "Get

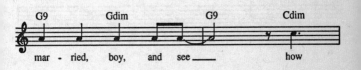

mar - ried, boy, and see __ how

hap - py you will be." __ I have looked all o -

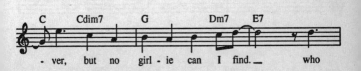

- ver, but no girl - ie can I find. __ who

I WISH I COULD SHIMMY LIKE MY SISTER KATE

Words and Music by
ARMAND J. PIRON

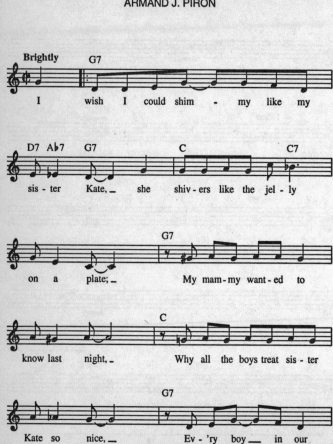

I wish I could shim - my like my sis - ter Kate, _ she shiv - ers like the jel - ly on a plate; _ My mam - my want - ed to know last night, _ Why all the boys treat sis - ter Kate so nice, _ Ev - 'ry boy _ in our

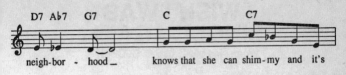

93

neigh-bor - hood __ knows that she can shim-my and it's

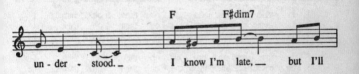

un - der - stood. __ I know I'm late, __ but I'll

be up to date __ when I can

shim - my like my sis - ter

Kate. I Kate, I mean,

shim - my like my sis - ter Kate. __

I WISH I WAS SINGLE AGAIN

Words and Music by J.C. BECKEL

1. I wish I was sin-gle, oh then, oh then, __ I wish I was sin-gle, oh then, _____ When I was sin-gle my pock-ets did jin-gle, And I wish I was sin-gle a-gain. _____
2. I mar-ried a wife, _ oh then, oh then, __ I mar-ried a wife, _ oh then, _____ I mar-ried a wife, she's the plague of my life, __ I __ wish I was sin-gle a-gain. _____
3. My wife __ took sick, _ oh then, oh then, __ My wife __ took sick, _ oh then, _____ My wife took sick, I went for the doc-tor right quick, _ I __ wish I was sin-gle a-gain. _____
4. My wife __ she died, _ oh then, oh then, __ My wife __ she died, _ oh then, _____ My wife she died, _ dang lit-tle cared I, _____ To __ think I was sin-gle a-gain. _____
5. I mar-ried an-oth-er, oh then, oh then, __ I mar-ried an-oth-er, oh then, _____ I mar-ried an-oth-er she's the Dev-il's step-moth-er And I wish I was sin-gle a-gain. _____
6. She beat me, she banged me, oh then, oh then, __ She beat me, she banged me, oh then, _____ She beat me, she banged me, she swore she would hang me, I __ wish I was sin-gle a-gain. _____
7. She got __ the rope, _ oh then, oh then, __ She got __ the rope, _ oh then, _____ She got the rope and she greased it with soap, _ And I wish I was sin-gle a-gain. _____

I WONDER WHO'S KISSING HER NOW

Lyrics by WILL M. HOUGH and FRANK R. ADAMS
Music by JOSEPH E. HOWARD and HAROLD ORLOB

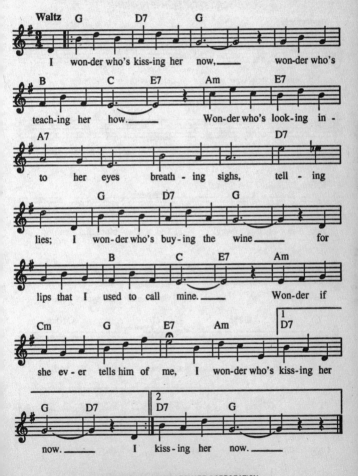

I'LL BUILD A STAIRWAY TO PARADISE

from GEORGE WHITE'S SCANDALS
from AN AMERICAN IN PARIS

Words by B.G. DeSYLVA and IRA GERSHWIN
Music by GEORGE GERSHWIN

IN MY MERRY OLDSMOBILE

Words by VINCENT BRYAN
Music by GUS EDWARDS

Waltz Tempo

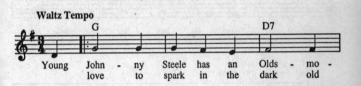

Young John - ny Steele has an Olds - mo -
love to spark in the dark old

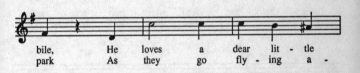

bile, He loves a dear lit - tle
park As they go fly - ing a -

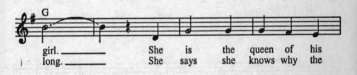

girl. _____ She is the queen of his
long. _____ She says she knows why the

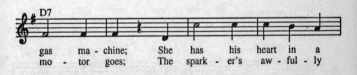

gas ma - chine; She has his heart in a
mo - tor goes; The spark - er's aw - ful - ly

whirl. _____ Now, when they go for a
strong. _____ Each day they spoon to the

spin, you know, She tries to learn the
en - gine's tune; Their hon - ey - moon will

au - to, so He lets her steer while he
hap - pen soon. He'll win Lu - cille with his

gets her ear, And whis - pers soft and
Olds - mo - bile And then he'll fond - ly

low;
croon: } Come a - way with me, Lu -

cille, _____ In my mer - ry Olds - mo -

bile, _____ Down the road of life we'll

fly Au - to - mo - bub - bling,

I'LL TAKE YOU HOME AGAIN, KATHLEEN

Words and Music by
THOMAS WESTENDORF

I'll take you home a-gain, Kath-leen, a-
know you love me, Kath-leen, dear, Your
that dear home be-yond the sea My

cross the o-cean wild and wide, To
heart was ev-er fond and true. I
Kath-leen shall a-gain re-turn, And

where your heart has ev-er been Since
al-ways feel when you are near That
when thy old friends wel-come thee, Thy

first you were my bon-ny bride. The
life holds noth-ing dear but you. The
lov-ing heart will cease to yearn. Where

ros-es all have left your cheek, I've
smiles that once you gave to me, I
laughs the lit-tle sil-ver stream, Be-

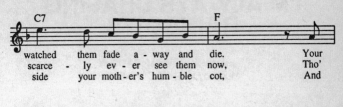

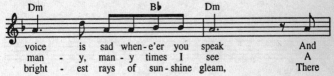

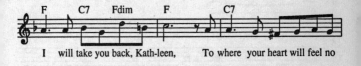

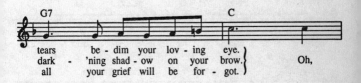

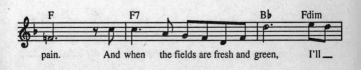

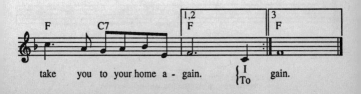

I'M ALWAYS CHASING RAINBOWS

Words by JOSEPH McCARTHY
Music by HARRY CARROLL

I'M JUST WILD
ABOUT HARRY

Words and Music by
NOBLE SISSLE and EUBIE BLAKE

IDA, SWEET AS APPLE CIDER

Words by EDDIE LEONARD
Music by EDDIE MUNSON

I - da, _____ sweet as ap - ple

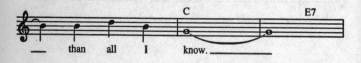

ci - der, _____ Sweet - er _____

_____ than all I know. _____

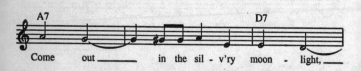

Come out _____ in the sil - v'ry moon - light, _____

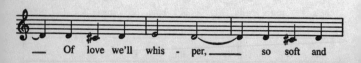

_____ Of love we'll whis - per, _____ so soft and

G7 C

low. _____ Seems I.

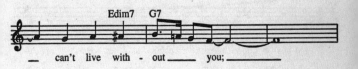

Edim7 G7

_ can't live with - out _____ you; _____

Dm   G7   C

Lis - ten, _____ oh hon - ey, do. _____

E7   A7

_ I da, _____ I i - dol -

D7   Dm7

ize you, _____ I love you, I - da.

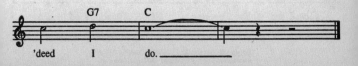

G7   C

'deed I do. _____

IF I HAD MY WAY

Words by LOU KLEIN
Music by JAMES KENDIS

Moderately

I'd like to make your gold-en dreams come true, dear, if
You'd nev-er know a care, a pain, or sor-row, if

I on-ly had my way, A par-a-dise this world would seem to
I on-ly had my way, I'd fill your cup of hap-pi-ness to-

you, ___ if I on-ly had my way. ___ } If
mor-row, if I on-ly had my way. ___ }

I had my way, dear, for-ev-er there'd

be a gar-den of ros-es for

you and for me. A thou-sand and

109

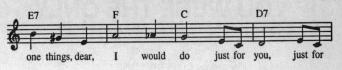

one things, dear, I would do just for you, just for

you, just for you. _____ If I had my

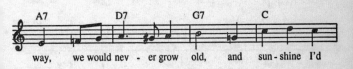

way, we would nev - er grow old, and sun - shine I'd

bring ev - 'ry day. _____ You would reign all a -

lone like a queen on a throne, if I

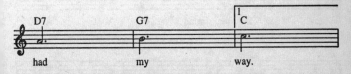

had my way.

If way. _____

IF YOU WERE THE ONLY GIRL IN THE WORLD

Words by CLIFFORD GREY
Music by NAT D. AYER

Slowly

If {you were / I was} the on - ly girl in the world, and {I was / you were} the on - ly boy, nothing else would mat - ter in the world to - day, we could go on lov - ing in the same old way. A Gar - den of E - den just made for

IN THE GOOD OLD SUMMERTIME

from IN THE GOOD OLD SUMMERTIME
from THE DEFENDER

Words by REN SHIELDS
Music by GEORGE EVANS

There's a time in each year that we al-ways hold
To swim in the pool you'd play "hook-ey" from

dear, Good old sum-mer-time,
school, Good old sum-mer-time,

With the birds and the trees and sweet scent-ed
You'd play "ring a-ros-ie" with Jim, Kate and

breez-es, Good old sum-mer-time,
Jo-sie, Good old sum-mer-time,

When your day's work is o-ver then you are in
Those days full of pleas-ure we now fond-ly

clo-ver, and life is one beau-ti-ful rhyme,
treas-ure, when we nev-er thought it a crime

No trou-ble an-noy-ing, each one is en-
To go steal-ing cher-ries, with face brown as

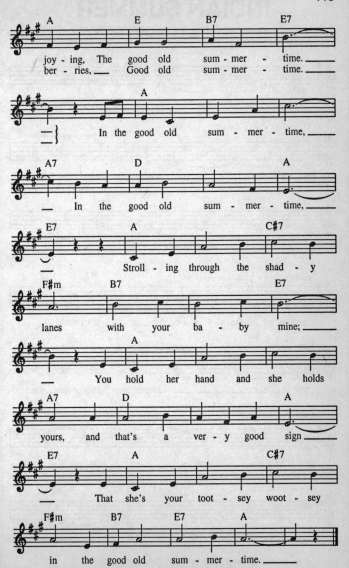

INDIAN SUMMER

Words and Music by VICTOR HERBERT

Slowly, with feeling

INDIANA
(Back Home Again in Indiana)

Words by BALLARD MacDONALD
Music by JAMES F. HANLEY

IT'S A LONG, LONG WAY
TO TIPPERARY

Words and Music by
JACK JUDGE and HARRY WILLIAMS

THE JAZZ-ME BLUES

Words and Music by
TOM DELANEY

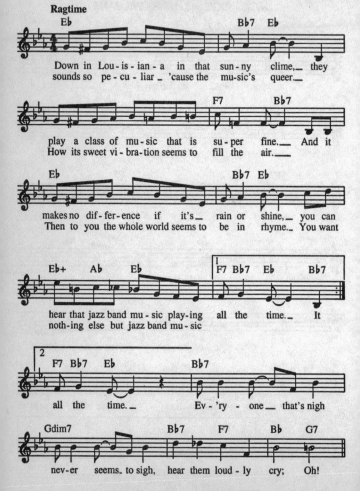

Down in Lou-is-ian-a in that sun-ny clime,_ they
sounds so pe-cu-liar _ 'cause the mu-sic's queer_

play a class of mu-sic that is su-per fine._ And it
How its sweet vi-bra-tion seems to fill the air._

makes no dif-fer-ence if it's_ rain or shine,_ you can
Then to you the whole world seems to be in rhyme._ You want

hear that jazz band mu-sic play-ing all the time._ It
noth-ing else but jazz band mu-sic

all the time._ Ev-'ry-one_ that's nigh

nev-er seems_ to sigh, hear them loud-ly cry; Oh!

JELLY ROLL BLUES

By FERDINAND "JELLY ROLL" MORTON

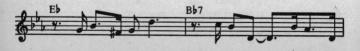

JOHNSON RAG

Words by JACK LAWRENCE
Music by GUY HALL and HENRY KLEINKAUF

Hep   Hep   There goes the John-son Rag — Hoy

Hoy   there goes the lat-est shag — Ho Ho   It real-ly

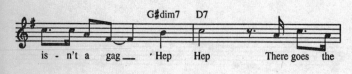

is - n't a gag — Hep   Hep   There goes the

John-son Rag — Jump   Jump   Don't let your

left foot drag — Jeep   Jeep   It's like a

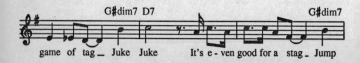

game of tag — Juke Juke   It's e-ven good for a stag — Jump

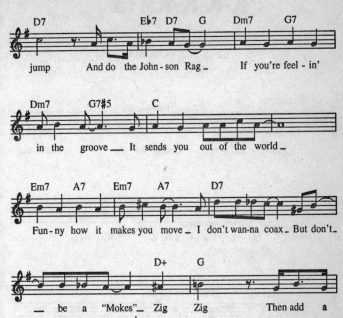

jump   And do the John-son Rag —   If you're feel-in'

in the   groove — It sends you   out of the world —

Fun-ny how it makes you   move — I don't wan-na coax — But don't—

— be   a   "Mokes" —   Zig   Zig   Then add   a

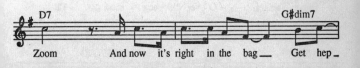

Zig Zig Sag — Zoop Zoop   Just let your shoul-ders wag — Zoom

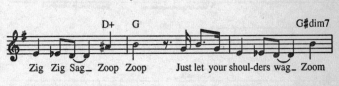

Zoom   And now it's right   in the   bag —   Get hep—

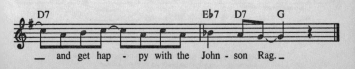

— and get hap - py with the   John - son Rag. —

K-K-K-KATY

Words and Music by
GEOFFREY O'HARA

K - K - K - Ka - ty,   beau-ti - ful Ka - ty,   You're the

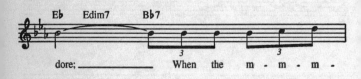

on - ly g - g - g - girl   that I   a -

dore; _____   When the m - m - m -

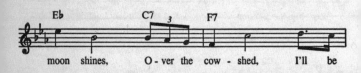

moon shines,   O - ver the cow - shed,   I'll be

wait - ing at the k - k - k-kitch - en door. ____

LET ME CALL YOU SWEETHEART

Music by BETH SLATER WHITSON
Music by LEO FRIEDMAN

LET THE REST OF THE WORLD GO BY

Words by J. KEIRN BRENNAN
Music by ERNEST R. BALL

Moderately, with expression

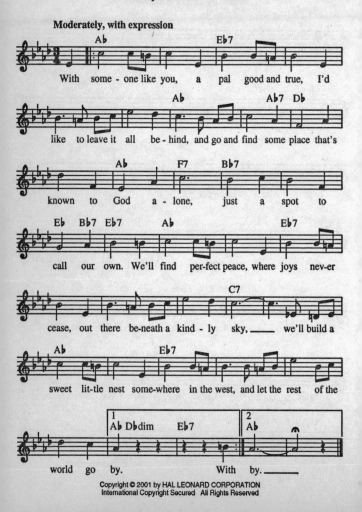

With some-one like you, a pal good and true, I'd
like to leave it all be-hind, and go and find some place that's
known to God a-lone, just a spot to
call our own. We'll find per-fect peace, where joys nev-er
cease, out there be-neath a kind-ly sky, ___ we'll build a
sweet lit-tle nest some-where in the west, and let the rest of the
world go by. With by. ___

MANDY

from YIP, YIP, YAPHANK
from ZIEGFELD FOLLIES

Words and Music by
IRVING BERLIN

Man - dy, _____ there's a min - is - ter hand - y. _____ And it sure would be dan - dy, _____ if we'd let him make a fee. _____ So don't you lin - ger, _____ here's the ring for your fin - ger. _____ Is - n't it a hum - din - ger? _____ Come a - long and let the wed - ding chimes bring hap - py times, for Man - dy and me. me.

LIMEHOUSE BLUES
from ZIEGFELD FOLLIES

Words by DOUGLAS FURBER
Music by PHILIP BRAHAM

Medium Swing

Oh Lime-house Kid, ___ oh oh oh Lime-house Kid, ___

___ go-ing the way ___ that the

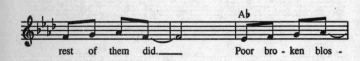

rest of them did. ___ Poor bro-ken blos-

- som and no-bod-y's child, ___

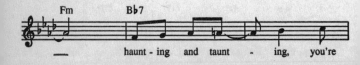

___ haunt-ing and taunt-ing, you're

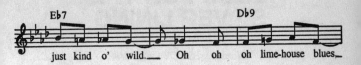

just kind o' wild.___ Oh oh oh lime-house blues,___

___ I've the real lime-house blues,___

Can't seem to shake___ off those sad Chi - na blues.___

___ Rings on your fin - gers and

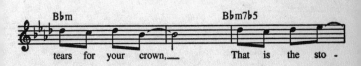

tears for your crown,___ That is the sto -

- ry of old Chi - na - town.___

LOOK FOR THE SILVER LINING

from SALLY

Words by BUDDY DeSYLVA
Music by JEROME KERN

heart full _____ of joy and

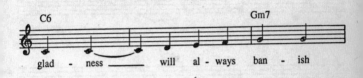

glad - ness _____ will al - ways ban - ish

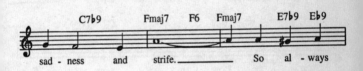

sad - ness and strife. _____ So al - ways

look for _____ the sil - ver

lin - ing _____ and try to find the

sun - ny side of life. _____

THE LOVE NEST

Words by OTTO HARBACH
Music by LOUIS A. HIRSCH

MA
(He's Making Eyes at Me)

Words by SIDNEY CLARE
Music by CON CONRAD

MAPLE LEAF RAG

Music by
SCOTT JOPLIN

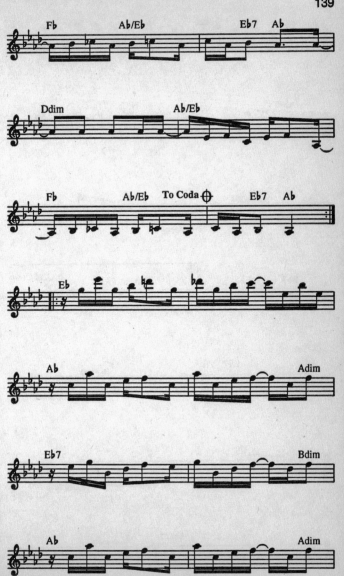

140

MARY'S A GRAND OLD NAME

from GEORGE M!
from FORTY-FIVE MINUTES FROM BROADWAY

Words and Music by
GEORGE M. COHAN

MARGIE

Words by BENNY DAVIS
Music by CON CONRAD and J. RUSSELL ROBINSON

Moderately, in 2

My lit - tle Mar - gie,

I'm al - ways think - ing of you,

Mar - gie, I'll tell the

world I love you, Don't for -

get your prom - ise to me, ___

___ I have bought a

MEET ME IN ST. LOUIS, LOUIS

from MEET ME IN ST. LOUIS

Words by ANDREW B. STERLING
Music by KERRY MILLS

Moderately

Meet me in St. Lou - is, Lou - is,

meet me at the fair. _____

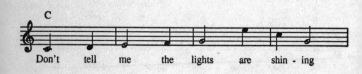

Don't tell me the lights are shin - ing

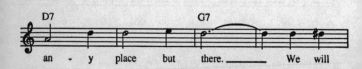

an - y place but there. _____ We will

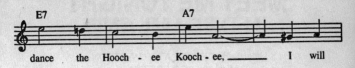

dance   the   Hooch - ee   Kooch - ee, _____   I   will

be   your   toots - ie   woots - ie; _____

Meet   me   in   St.   Lou - is,   Lou - is,

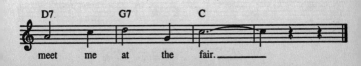

meet   me   at   the   fair. _____

MEET ME TONIGHT IN DREAMLAND

Words by BETH SLATER WHITSON
Music by LEO FRIEDMAN

MELODY OF LOVE

By H. ENGELMANN

MEMORIES

Words by GUS KAHN
Music by EGBERT VAN ALSTYNE

Slowly

Mem - o - ries, mem - o - ries,

Dreams of love so true,___ O'er the

sea of mem - o - ry I'm drift - ing back to

you.___ Child - hood days,

wild - wood days, A - mong the birds and bees,___

— You left me a - lone But still, you're my

own in my beau - ti - ful mem - o - ries.___

MOONLIGHT BAY

Words by EDWARD MADDEN
Music by PERCY WENRICH

M-O-T-H-E-R
(A Word That Means the World to Me)

Words by HOWARD JOHNSON
Music by THEODORE MORSE

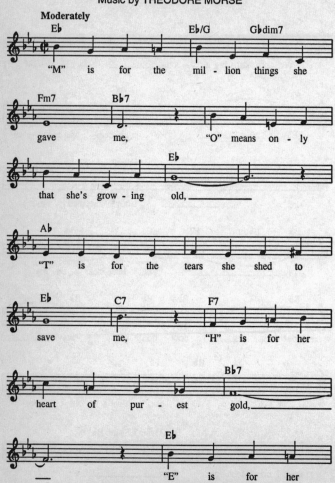

Moderately

Eb — "M" is for the mil - lion things she

Eb/G   Gbdim7

Fm7   Bb7 — gave me, "O" means on - ly

that she's grow - ing old, _____ Eb

Ab — "T" is for the tears she shed to

Eb   C7   F7 — save me, "H" is for her

heart of pur - est gold, _____ Bb7

Eb — "E" is for her

MY BUDDY

Lyrics by GUS KAHN
Music by WALTER DONALDSON

Dedicated to my friend "Private Howard Friend"
who occupies the cot next to mine and feels as I do about the "bugler"

OH! HOW I HATE TO GET UP IN THE MORNING

from the Stage Production YIP, YIP, YAPHANK
from the Stage Production THIS IS THE ARMY

Words and Music by IRVING BERLIN

The oth-er day I chanced to meet a
bu-gler in the ar-my is the

sol-dier friend of mine. _____ He'd
luck-i-est of men, _____ He

been in camp for sev-'ral weeks and
wakes the boys at five and then goes

he was look-ing fine. _____ His
back to bed a-gain. _____ He

mus-cles had de-vel-oped and his
does-n't have to blow a-gain un-

cheeks were ros-y red. I
til the af-ter-noon. If

MY HERO

Words by STANISLAUS STANGE
Music by OSCAR STRAUS

MY MAN
(Mon Homme)
from ZIEGFELD FOLLIES

Words by ALBERT WILLEMETZ and JACQUES CHARLES
English Words by CHANNING POLLOCK
Music by MAURICE YVAIN

It's cost me a lot, but there's one thing that I've got, it's
Some-times I say, if I just could get a-way with

my man. Cold and wet, tired you bet, but all
my man, he'd go straight, sure as fate, for it

that I soon for-get with _ my man. He's
nev-er is too late for _ a man. I

not much for looks and no he-ro out of books is
just like to dream of a cot-tage by a stream with

my man. Two or three girls has he that he
my man, where a few flow-ers grew and per-

likes as well as me, but I love him. I _____
haps a kid or two like _ my man. And _____

don't know why I should, he is-n't good,
then my eyes get wet, I 'most for-get,

161

MY MELANCHOLY BABY

Words by GEORGE NORTON
Music by ERNIE BURNETT

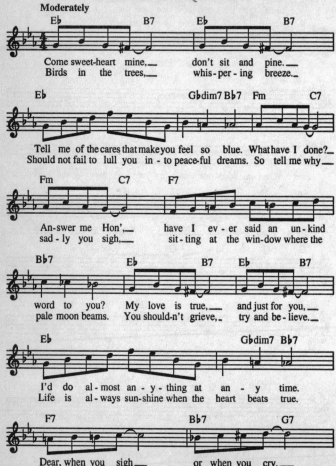

Come sweet-heart mine,_ don't sit and pine._
Birds in the trees,_ whis-per-ing breeze._

Tell me of the cares that make you feel so blue. What have I done?
Should not fail to lull you in-to peace-ful dreams. So tell me why_

An-swer me Hon',_ have I ev-er said an un-kind
sad-ly you sigh,_ sit-ting at the win-dow where the

word to you? My love is true,_ and just for you,_
pale moon beams. You should-n't grieve,_ try and be-lieve._

I'd do al-most an-y-thing at an-y time.
Life is al-ways sun-shine when the heart beats true.

Dear, when you sigh_ or when you cry,_
Be of good cheer,_ smile thro' your tears,_

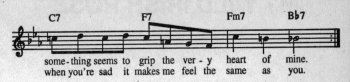

C7   F7   Fm7   Bb7

some-thing seems to grip the ver - y heart of mine.
when you're sad it makes me feel the same as you.

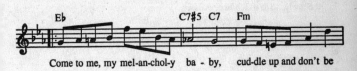

Eb   C7#5 C7 Fm

Come to me, my mel-an-chol-y ba - by, cud-dle up and don't be

Bb7   F7 Bb7

blue;   All your fears are fool-ish fan-cy, may - be,

Eb   Edim7 Bb7

you know, dear, that I'm in love with you.

Eb   C7#5 C7 Fm

Ev-'ry cloud must have a sil-ver lin - ing, wait un-til the sun shines

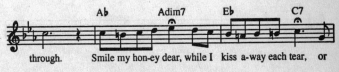

Ab   Adim7   Eb   C7

through.   Smile my hon-ey dear, while I kiss a-way each tear, or

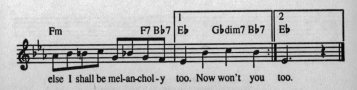

Fm   F7 Bb7   1. Eb   Gbdim7 Bb7   2. Eb

else I shall be mel-an-chol-y too. Now won't you too.

MY WILD IRISH ROSE

Words and Music by
CHAUNCEY OLCOTT

165

OH JOHNNY,
OH JOHNNY, OH!

Words by ED ROSE
Music by ABE OLMAN

OH! YOU
BEAUTIFUL DOLL

Words by A. SEYMOUR BROWN
Music by NAT D. AYER

OVER THERE

Words and Music by
GEORGE M. COHAN

PACK UP YOUR TROUBLES IN YOUR OLD KIT BAG AND SMILE, SMILE, SMILE

Words by GEORGE ASAF
Music by FELIX POWELL

March tempo

Pack up your trou-bles in your old kit bag and smile,

smile, smile. ____ While you've a lu-ci-fer to

light your fag. Smile, boys, that's the style. ____

What's the use of wor-ry-ing? ____ It nev-er

was worth-while. So, pack up your trou-bles in your

old kit bag and smile, smile, smile. ____

PAPER DOLL

Words and Music by
JOHNNY S. BLACK

Reflectively

I'm goin' to buy a pa-per doll that I can call my own, a doll that oth-er fel-lows can-not steal and then the flir-ty, flir-ty guys with their flir-ty, flir-ty eyes, will have to flirt with dol-lies that are real. When I come home at night she will be wait-ing, __ She'll be the tru-est doll in all this world. I'd rath-er have a pa-per doll to call my own, than have a fick-le-mind-ed real live girl. I'm goin' to girl. __

PEG O' MY HEART

Words by ALFRED BRYAN
Music by FRED FISHER

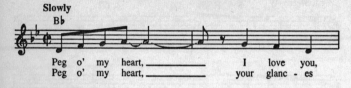

Peg o' my heart, _____ I love you,
Peg o' my heart, _____ your glanc - es

don't let us part, _____ I love you.
make my heart say, _____ "How's chanc - es."

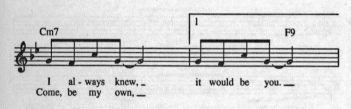

I al - ways knew, _ it would be you. _
Come, be my own, _

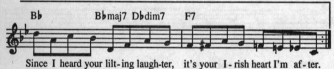

Since I heard your lilt - ing laugh - ter, it's your I - rish heart I'm af - ter.

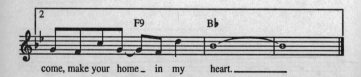

come, make your home _ in my heart. _____

PRETTY BABY

Words by GUS KAHN
Music by EGBERT VAN ALSTYNE
and TONY JACKSON

Ev-'ry-bod-y loves a ba-by that's why I'm in love with you, pret-ty

ba - by, pret - ty ba - by, and I'd

like to be your sis - ter, broth - er, dad and moth - er too, pret - ty

ba - by, pret - ty ba - by. Won't you

come and let me rock you in my cra - dle of love,__ and we'll

cud - dle all the time.__ Oh! I want a lov-in' ba - by and it

might as well be you, pret - ty ba - by of mine.

PLAY A SIMPLE MELODY

from the Stage Production WATCH YOUR STEP

Words and Music by
IRVING BERLIN

Won't you play a sim-ple mel - o-

dy like my moth-er sang to

me, _____ one with

good old fash-ioned har - mo - ny.

Play a sim-ple mel-o-dy.

Mus-i-cal de - mon, set your

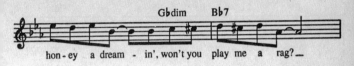

hon - ey a dream - in', won't you play me a rag?

Just change that clas - si - cal nag

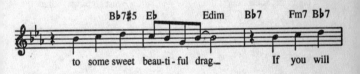

to some sweet beau - ti - ful drag If you will

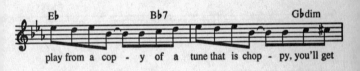

play from a cop - y of a tune that is chop - py, you'll get

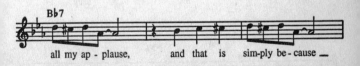

all my ap - plause, and that is sim - ply be - cause

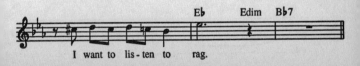

I want to lis - ten to rag.

176

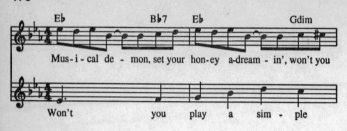

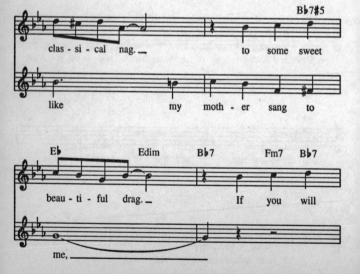

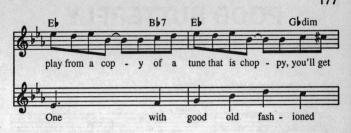

play from a cop - y of a tune that is chop - py, you'll get

One with good old fash - ioned

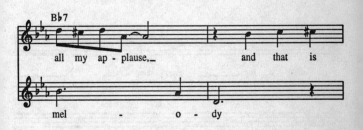

all my ap - plause,— and that is

mel - o - dy

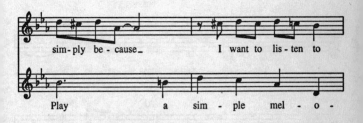

sim - ply be - cause— I want to lis - ten to

Play a sim - ple mel - o -

rag._____

dy._____

POOR BUTTERFLY

Words by JOHN L. GOLDEN
Music by RAYMOND HUBBELL

Slowly, with much expression

Poor but-ter-fly _____ 'neath the blos-soms wait-ing, _____ poor but-ter-fly _____ for she loved him so. _____ The mo-ments pass in-to hours, _____ the hours _____ pass in-to years, _____ and as she smiles through her tears, _____

A PRETTY GIRL
IS LIKE A MELODY

from the 1919 Stage Production ZIEGFELD FOLLIES
from THE GREAT ZIEGFELD

Words and Music by
IRVING BERLIN

PUT YOUR ARMS
AROUND ME, HONEY

Words by JUNIE McCREE
Music by ALBERT VON TILZER

Moderately bright

Put your arms a-round me, hon-ey, hold me
When they look at me,__ my heart be - gins__ to

tight. Hud - dle up and cud - dle up with
float. Then it starts a-rock - in' like a

all __ your might. Oh!
mo - tor boat. Oh!

Oh! Won't you roll those eyes. __
Oh!

Eyes that I just i-dol-ize.__

I nev-er knew __ an-y { girl
{ boy

like you.

ROCK-A-BYE YOUR BABY
WITH A DIXIE MELODY
from SINBAD
Words by SAM M. LEWIS and JOE YOUNG
Music by JEAN SCHWARTZ

G7   C

love that's   in ___   ya.   "Weep   No   More,   My

C/E   E♭dim7   Dm7   G7

La-dy;"   sing ___   that   song   a - gain   for   me,   And

Dm7   G7   Dm7   G7   F7

"Old   Black   Joe," ___   just   as   though ___   you

E7

had _____   me   on   your   knee.

A7

A   mil-lion   ba - by   kiss - es   I'll   de - li -   ver

D7   D#dim7

the   min - ute   that   you   sing   the   "Swan-ee   Riv - er;"

C/E   C   E7/G#   Am

rock - a - bye   your   rock - a - bye   ba - by   with   a

D7   G7   C

Dix - ie   mel - o -   dy.

ROSE ROOM

Words by HARRY WILLIAMS
Music by ART HICKMAN

ROSES OF PICARDY

Words by FRED E. WEATHERLY
Music by HAYDN WOOD

ROW, ROW, ROW

Words by WILLIAM JEROME
Music by JIMMIE V. MONACO

And then he'd row, row, row, way up the
riv-er he would row, row, row, a hug he'd
give her then he'd kiss her now and then. She would tell him
when, he'd fool a-round and fool a-round and then they'd kiss a-
gain. And then he'd row, row, row, a lit-tle
fur-ther he would row, oh, oh, oh, oh.
Then he'd drop both his oars, take a few more en-cores,
and then he'd row, row, row.

ROYAL GARDEN BLUES

Words and Music by CLARENCE WILLIAMS
and SPENCER WILLIAMS

Moderate Swing

No use of talk-in' no use of talk-in'. You'll

start in dog-walk-in' no mat-ter where

there's jazz-co-pa-tion, blues mod-u-la-tion.

Just like a Hait-ian you'll rip and tear,

most ev-'ry-bod-y likes the

blues. Here's why I'm rav-in'

here's why I'm rav-in' if it's blues you are crav-in' just

THE SHEIK OF ARABY

Words by HARRY B. SMITH and FRANCIS WHEELER
Music by TED SNYDER

ST. JAMES INFIRMARY

Words and Music by
JOE PRIMROSE

Slow Blues tempo

I went down to the St. James In- firm- 'ry to
down to old Joe's bar- room, on the

see my ba- by there. She was
cor- ner by the square; they were

ly- in' on a long white ta- ble, so
serv- in' the drinks as u- sual, and the

sweet, so cool, so fair. 2. Went
u- su- al crowd was there. 4. On my

up to see the doc- tor. "She's ver- y low," he
left stood Joe Mc- Ken- ne- dy, his eyes blood- shot

said. Went back to see my ba- by; great
red; he turned to the crowd a- round him, these

God! She was ly- in' there dead. 3. I went
are the words he said: 5. Let her

go, let her go, God bless her, wher -
gam - blers to car - ry my cof - fin, six

ev - er she may be; she may
cho - rus girls to sing my song; put a

search this wide world o - ver, she'll __
jazz band on my tail - gate to raise

nev - er find a man like me. 6. Oh, when I die please
hell as we go __ a - long. 8. Now that's the end of my

bur - y me in my high - top Stet - son hat; put a
sto - ry; let's have an - oth - er round of booze. And if

gold piece on my watch chain so they'll
an - y - one should ask you, just tell them I've got the

know I died __ stand - in' pat. 7. Get six
St. James In - fir - ma - ry Blues.

ST. LOUIS BLUES

from BIRTH OF THE BLUES

Words and Music by
W.C. HANDY

I'll pack my trunk, ___ make my get - a -

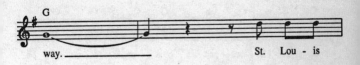

way. _____ St. Lou - is

wom - an, ___ with her dia - mond

rings, _____ pulls that man 'round ___

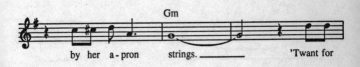

by her a - pron strings. ____ 'Twant for

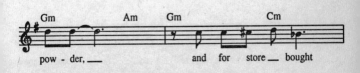

pow - der, ___ and for store ___ bought

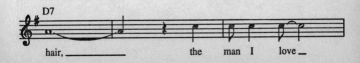

hair, _____ the man I love ___

Additional Lyrics

2. Been to the Gypsy to get my fortune told,
   To the Gypsy, to get my fortune told.
   'Cause I'm most wild about my jelly roll.

   Gypsy done told me: "Don't you wear no black,"
   Yes she done told me: "Don't you wear no black,"
   Go to St. Louis, you can win him back.

   Help me to Cairo, make St. Louis by myself,
   Gone to Cairo, find my old friend Jeff.
   Goin' to pin myself close to his side,
   If I flag his train, I sure can ride.

   I love that man like a schoolboy loves his pie,
   Like a Kentucky Colonel loves his mint and rye.
   I'll love my baby till the day I die.

3. You ought to see that stovepipe brown of mine,
   Like he owns the diamond Joseph line.
   He'd make a cross-eyed old man go stone blind.

   Blacker than midnight, teeth like flags of truce,
   Blackest man in the whole St. Louis.
   Blacker the berry, sweeter is the juice.

   About a crap game, he knows a powerful lot,
   But when work time comes, he's on the dot,
   Goin' to ask him for a cold ten spot,
   What it takes to get it, he's certainly got.

   A black-headed gal make a freight train jump the track,
   Said a black-headed gal make a freight train jump the track.
   But a red-headed woman makes a preacher ball the jack.

SAY IT WITH MUSIC

from the 1921 Stage Production MUSIC BOX REVUE
from the 20th Century Fox Motion Picture
ALEXANDER'S RAGTIME BAND
Words and Music by
IRVING BERLIN

Eb/Bb   Abm   Gbm6/A   Cb7/A

sic,   Some - how   they'd

Eb/Bb   Ab   Eb/G

rath - er   be   kissed ___   to   the

Bdim   Cm   F7   Bb7

strains   of   Cho - pin   or   Liszt. ___   A

Eb   Bb7   Bb7/F

mel - o - dy   mel - low

Ab   Eb   G7

played   on   a   cel - lo

Bbm   Gm7b5   C7   Edim   Fm

helps   Mis - ter   Cu - pid   a - long. ___

Fm/Ab   C/G   Fm7   Fm7b5   Bb7

___   So   say   it   with   a   beau - ti - ful   song. ___

1
Eb   F Bb7

2
Eb   Db7/Ab   B7/Gb   Bb7/F   Eb

SECOND HAND ROSE

Words by GRANT CLARKE
Music by JAMES F. HANLEY

never get a single thing that's new. ____
never get what other girl-ies do. ____

____ E - ven Jake the plumb - er, he's the
____ Once while stroll - ing through the Ritz a

man I a - dore, ____ had the nerve to
girl got my goat, ____ she nudged her friend and

tell me he's been mar - ried be - fore. ____
said, "Oh! look, there's my old fur coat." ____

Ev - 'ry - one knows ____ that I'm just Sec - ond Hand Rose ____
Ev - 'ry - one knows ____ that I'm just Sec - ond Hand Rose ____

____ from Sec - ond Av - e - nue.
____ from Sec - ond Av - e -

I'm wear - ing nue. ____

SHINE ON, HARVEST MOON

Words by JACK NORWORTH
Music by NORA BAYES and JACK NORWORTH

SIDEWALKS OF NEW YORK

Words and Music by CHARLES B. LAWLOR
and JAMES W. BLAKE

SILVER THREADS AMONG THE GOLD

Words by EBEN E. REXFORD
Music by HART P. DANKS

Darling, I am grow-ing old, _____
When your hair is sil-ver white, ____
Love can nev-er more grow old, ____
Love is al-ways young and fair; ____

Sil- ver threads a-mong the gold
And your cheeks no long-er bright
Locks may lose their brown and gold,
What to us is sil-ver hair,

Shine up-on my brow to-day; ____
With the ros-es of the May, ____
Cheeks may fade and hol-low grow, ____
Fad- ed cheeks or steps grown slow, ____

Life is fast fad-ing a-way.
I will kiss your lips and say:
But the hearts that love will know;
To the hearts that beat be-low?

But, my dar-ling, you will be, will be,
Oh, my dar-ling, mine a-lone, a-lone,
Nev- er, nev-er win-ter's frost can chill,
Since I kissed you, mine a-lone, a-lone,

SMILES

Words by J. WILL CALLAHAN
Music by LEE S. ROBERTS

There are smiles____ that make us hap - py,____ there are smiles ____ that make us blue, ____ there are smiles that steal a - way the tear - drops____ as the sun - beams steal a - way the dew, ____ there are smiles that have a ten - der mean - ing ____ that the eyes of love a - lone may see, ____ and the smiles that fill my life with sun - shine ____ are the smiles that you give to me. ____

THE SWEETHEART OF SIGMA CHI

Words by BYRON D. STOKES
Music by F. DUDLEIGH VERNOR

The girl of my dreams is the sweet-est girl of all the girls I know. _____ Each sweet co-ed, like a rain-bow trail, fades in the af-ter-glow. _____ The blue of her eyes and the gold of her hair, are a blend of the west-ern sky; _____ And the moon-light beams on the girl of my dreams, she's the sweet-heart of Sig-ma Chi. _____

SOMEBODY STOLE MY GAL

Words and Music by
LEO WOOD

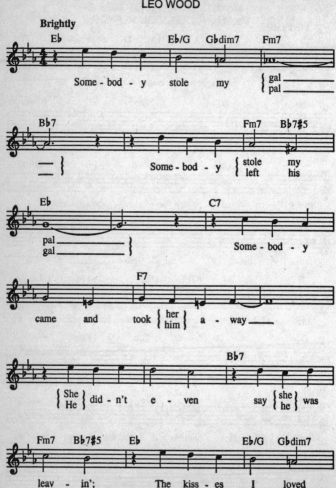

SUGAR BLUES

Words by LUCY FLETCHER
Music by CLARENCE WILLIAMS

Moderate Blues tempo

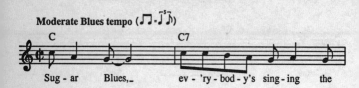

Sug - ar Blues, ev - 'ry-bod - y's sing-ing the

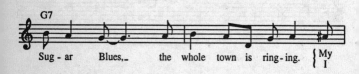

Sug - ar Blues,_ the whole town is ring-ing. {My I

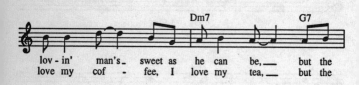

lov - in' man's_ sweet as he can be,_ but the
love my cof - fee, I love my tea,_ but the

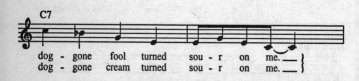

dog - gone fool turned sou - r on me._ __
dog - gone cream turned sou - r on me._ __ }

I'm so un - hap - py, I feel so bad _ I could

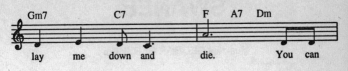

lay   me   down and   die.   You can

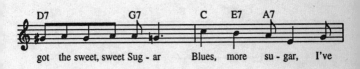

say what you choose _ but I'm all con - fused, I've

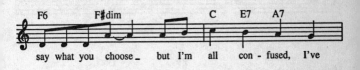

got the sweet, sweet Sug - ar   Blues,   more   su - gar,   I've

got the sweet, sweet Sug - ar   Blues. _____ I've got the

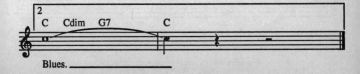

Blues. _____

SWANEE

Words by IRVING CAESAR
Music by GEORGE GERSHWIN

SWEETHEARTS
from SWEETHEARTS

Words by ROBERT B. SMITH
Music by VICTOR HERBERT

Sweet-hearts make love their ver - y own,

sweet-hearts can live on love a - lone.

For them the eyes where love - light lies

o - pen the gates to Par - a - dise!

All oth - er love is doomed to fade, It is like

sun - shine veiled in shade. Such joys of

life as love im - parts are all of them

yours, sweet - hearts! _____

THAT'S A PLENTY

Words by RAY GILBERT
Music by LEW POLLACK

That's a plen - ty's got - ta beat in it the
Dix - ie - land comes ooz - in' out of it, the

rhy - thm's got a lot of heat in it,
Dix - ie - land - ers sure are proud of it, they

bet - cha five, ten to five, it's
call it jazz, what it has,

gon - na get - cha do - in' what it's do - in' to me. The

that's a plen - ty for me. It

takes you down to New Or - leans, down
Shut my big brown roll - ing eyes, if

Ba - sin Street with all the queens. You don't have to
you don't rock - et to the skies,

TAKE ME OUT
TO THE BALL GAME
from TAKE ME OUT TO THE BALL GAME

Words by JACK NORWORTH
Music by ALBERT VON TILZER

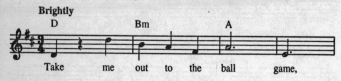

Take me out to the ball game,

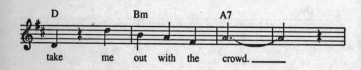

take me out with the crowd. _____

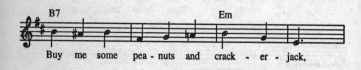

Buy me some pea-nuts and crack-er-jack,

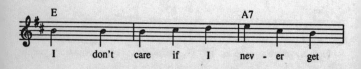

I don't care if I nev-er get

back. Let me root, root, root for the

Home team, If they don't win it's a

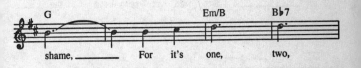

shame, _____ For it's one, two,

three strikes, you're out at the old ball

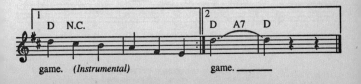

game. *(Instrumental)*　　　game. _____

THEY DIDN'T BELIEVE ME
from THE GIRL FROM UTAH

Words by HERBERT REYNOLDS
Music by JEROME KERN

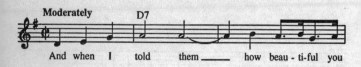

And when I told them _____ how beau-ti-ful you

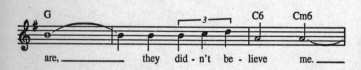

are, _____ they did-n't be-lieve me. _____

_____ They did-n't be-lieve me! _____ Your lips, your

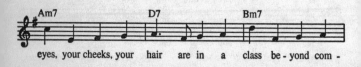

eyes, your cheeks, your hair are in a class be-yond com-

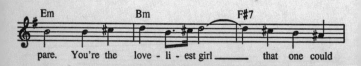

pare. You're the love-li-est girl _____ that one could

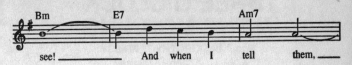

Bm E7 Am7

see! _____ And when I tell them, ___

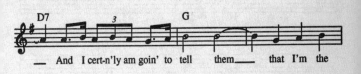

D7 _3_ G

__ And I cert-n'ly am goin' to tell them___ that I'm the

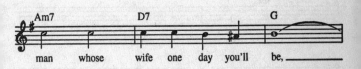

Am7 D7 G

man whose wife one day you'll be, _____

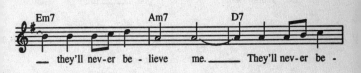

Em7 Am7 D7

__ they'll nev-er be - lieve me. _____ They'll nev-er be -

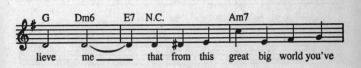

G Dm6 E7 N.C. Am7

lieve me ___ that from this great big world you've

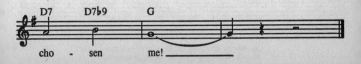

D7 D7b9 G

cho - sen me! _____

THREE O'CLOCK
IN THE MORNING

Words by DOROTHY TERRISS
Music by JULIAN ROBLEDO

TIGER RAG
(Hold That Tiger)

Words by HARRY DeCOSTA
Music by ORIGINAL DIXIELAND JAZZ BAND

Where's that ti - ger! Where's that ti - ger!

Where's that ti - ger! Where's that ti - ger!

Hold that ti - ger! Hold that ti - ger!

Hold that ti - ger! Choke him, poke him, kick him and soak him!

Where's that ti - ger? Where's that ti - ger?

Where, ___ oh where can he be? ___ Low or

High - brow, they all cry now: "Please play that

Ti - ger Rag for me." ___ me." ___

TILL WE MEET AGAIN

Words by RAYMOND B. EGAN
Music by RICHARD A. WHITING

Smile the while you kiss me sad a - dieu.
Wed - ding bells will ring so mer - ri - ly,

When the clouds roll by, I'll come to you.
ev - 'ry tear will be a mem - o - ry so

Then the skies will seem more blue.
wait and pray each night for me

Down in lov - er's lane my dear - ie,

till we meet a - gain.

TOO-RA-LOO-RA-LOO-RAL

(That's an Irish Lullaby)

from GOING MY WAY

Words and Music by
JAMES R. SHANNON

Moderately, with expression

Too - ra-loo - ra - loo-ral, ___ too - ra-loo - ra - li,

too - ra-loo - ra - loo-ral, ___ hush now, don't you

cry! ___ Too - ra-loo - ra - loo-ral, ___

too - ra-loo - ra - li, too - ra-loo - ra -

loo-ral, that's an I - rish lull - a - by.

TOOT, TOOT, TOOTSIE!

(Good-bye!)

from THE JAZZ SINGER

Words and Music by GUS KAHN, ERNIE ERDMAN,
DAN RUSSO and TED FIORITO

TWELFTH STREET RAG

By EUDAY L. BOWMAN

231

THE WABASH CANNON BALL

American Hobo Song, circa 1880s

1. From the great At-lan-tic O-cean to the
2. Lis-ten to the rhyth-mic jin-gle and the
3. She was com-ing from At-lan-ta on a

wide Pa-cif-ic's shore, From the ones we leave be-
rum-ble and the roar, As she glides a-long the
cold De-cem-ber day. As she rolled in-to the

hind us to the ones we see once
wood-lands through the hills and by the
sta-tion, I could hear a wom-an

more. She's might-y tall and hand-some, and
shore. You hear the might-y en-gine and
say: "He's might-y big and hand-some, and

quite well known by all, How we love the
pray that it won't stall, While we safe-ly
sure did make me fall, He's a-com-ing

choo choo of the Wa-bash Can-non-
trav-el on the Wa-bash Can-non-
tow'rd me on the Wa-bash Can-non-

ball.
ball.
ball."

Hear the bell and whis- tle call- ing, Hear the wheels that go "clack clack", Hear the roar- ing of the en- gine, As she rolls a- long the track. The mag- ic of the rail- road wins hearts of one and all, As we reach our des- tin- a- tion on the Wa- bash Can- non- ball.

WAIT 'TIL THE SUN SHINES, NELLIE

Words by ANDREW B. STERLING
Music by HARRY VON TILZER

—   We'll   face   the

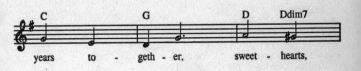

years   to - geth - er,   sweet - hearts,

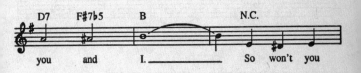

you   and   I. _____   So   won't   you

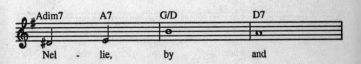

wait   till   the   sun   shines,

Nel - lie,   by   and

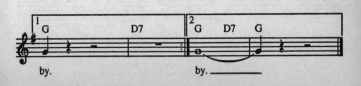

by.   by. _____

WAITING FOR THE ROBERT E. LEE

Words by L. WOLFE GILBERT
Music by LEWIS F. MUIR

'Way down on the lev - ee, In
The whis - tles are blow - in', The

old Al - a - bam - y, There's
smoke - stacks are show - in', The

dad - dy and mam - my, There's
ropes they are throw - in'; Ex -

E - phra'm and Sam - my; On a
cuse me, I'm go - in' to the

moon - light night you can find __
place where all is har - mo -

— them all; While they are wait - in', The
— ni - ous; E - ven the preach - er, They

237

Watch them shuf - flin' a - long; See them shuf - flin' a - long. Go take your best gal, real pal, Go down to the lev - ee, I said to the lev - ee! And then

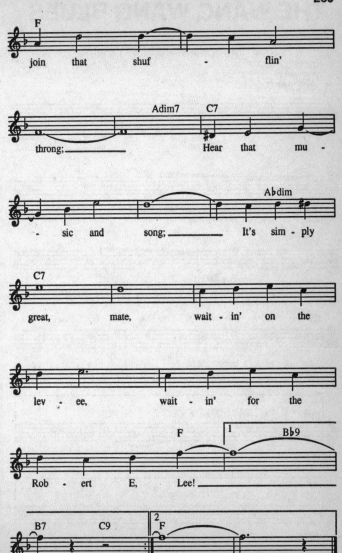

THE WANG WANG BLUES

**Words and Music by LEO WOOD, GUS MUELLER,
BUSTER JOHNSON and HENRY BUSSE**

WHEN MY BABY SMILES AT ME

Words and Music by HARRY VON TILZER,
ANDREW B. STERLING, BILL MUNRO and TED LEWIS

'WAY DOWN YONDER IN NEW ORLEANS

Words and Music by HENRY CREAMER
and J. TURNER LAYTON

Moderate bounce

'Way down yon - der in New Or - leans

in the land of dream - y scenes

there's a gar - den of E - den

that's what I mean. Cre-ole ba - bies with

flash - ing eyes soft - ly whis - per with

ten - der sighs, "Stop! Oh! won't you

WHEN IRISH EYES ARE SMILING

Words by CHAUNCEY OLCOTT and GEORGE GRAFF, JR.
Music by ERNEST R. BALL

Moderately, with expression

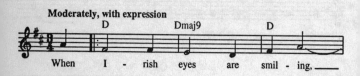

When I - rish eyes are smil - ing, ____

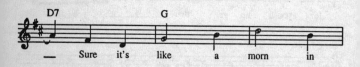

____ Sure it's like a morn in

Spring. ____ In the lilt of

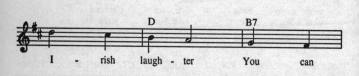

I - rish laugh - ter You can

hear the an - gels sing. ____

245

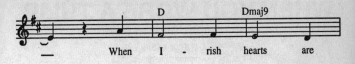

When I - rish hearts are

hap - py, _____ All the world seems

bright and gay, _____ And when

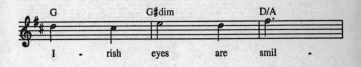

I - rish eyes are smil -

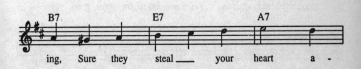

ing, Sure they steal ___ your heart a -

way. When way. _____

WHEN YOU WORE A TULIP
(And I Wore a Big Red Rose)

Words by JACK MAHONEY
Music by PERCY WENRICH

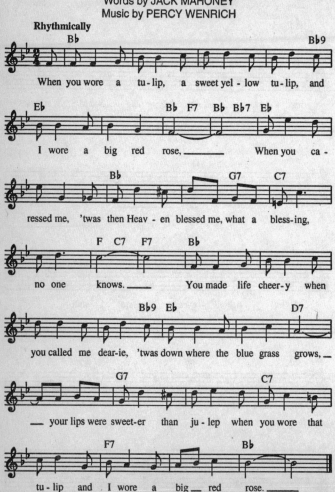

WHISPERING

Words and Music by RICHARD COBURN,
JOHN SCHONBERGER and VINCENT ROSE

THE YELLOW ROSE OF TEXAS

Traditional Folksong

1. There's a yel - low rose in Tex - as That I am goin' to see, No oth - er fel - low loves her, No - bod - y, on - ly me. She cried so when I left her, It like to broke my heart. And if I ev - er find her, We nev - er - more will find her,

2. Where the Ri - o Grande is flow - ing And the star - ry skies are bright, She walks a - long the riv - er In the qui - et sum - mer night. She thinks, if I re - mem - ber, When we part - ed long a - go, I prom - ised to come back a - gain And not to leave her

3. Oh, now I'm goin' to find her For my heart is full of woe, And we'll sing the song to - geth - er, That we sang so long a - go. We'll play the ban - jo gai - ly And we'll sing the songs of yore. And the Yel - low Rose of Tex - as Shall be mine for - ev - er -

YOU MADE ME LOVE YOU
(I Didn't Want to Do It)
from BROADWAY MELODY OF 1938

Words by JOE McCARTHY
Music by JAMES V. MONACO

251

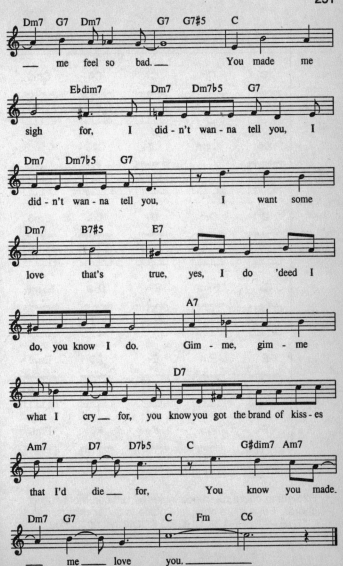

GUITAR CHORD FRAMES

	C	Cm	C+	C6	Cm6
C					

	C#	C#m	C#+	C#6	C#m6
C#/Db					

	D	Dm	D+	D6	Dm6
D					

	Eb	Ebm	Eb+	Eb6	Ebm6
Eb/D#					

	E	Em	E+	E6	Em6
E					

	F	Fm	F+	F6	Fm6
F					

This guitar chord reference includes 120 commonly used chords. For a more complete guide to guitar chords, see "THE PAPERBACK CHORD BOOK" (HL00702009).

	C7	Cmaj7	Cm7	C7sus	Cdim7
C					

	C#7	C#maj7	C#m7	C#7sus	C#dim7
C#/Db					

	D7	Dmaj7	Dm7	D7sus	Ddim7
D					

	Eb7	Ebmaj7	Ebm7	Eb7sus	Ebdim7
Eb/D#					

	E7	Emaj7	Em7	E7sus	Edim7
E					

	F7	Fmaj7	Fm7	F7sus	Fdim7
F					

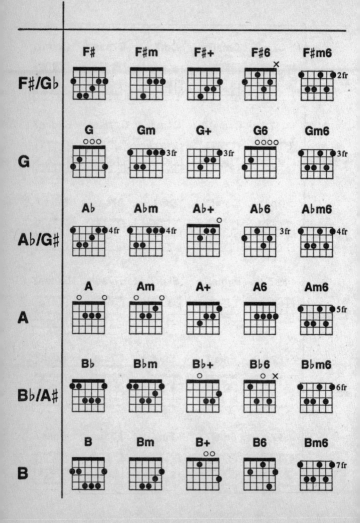